FastTrack
MUSIC INSTRUCTION

Harmonica 1

INTRODUCTION

Welcome back to FastTrack®!

Hope you enjoyed *Harmonica 1* and are ready to play some hits. Have you and your friends formed a band? Or do you feel like soloing along with the audio tracks? Either way, make sure you're relaxed…it's time to jam!

The eight songs in this book are all for C diatonic harmonica. With the knowledge you already have, you're ready to play them. But it's still important to remember the three Ps: **patience**, **practice**, and **pace yourself**.

As with *Harmonica 1*, don't try to bite off more than you can chew. If you're tired, take some time off. If you get frustrated, put down your harp, relax, and just listen to the tracks. If you forget something, go back and relearn it. If you're doing fine, think about charging admission.

CONTENTS

T0195162

ABOUT THE AUDIO

Again, you get audio tracks with the book! Each song in the book is included, so you can hear how it sounds and play along when you're ready.

Each audio example is preceded by one measure of "clicks" to indicate the tempo and meter. Pan right to hear the harmonica part emphasized. Pan left to hear the accompaniment part emphasized.

To access audio visit:
www.halleonard.com/mylibrary

Enter Code
5659-9421-6350-0076

ISBN 978-0-634-02074-2

HAL•LEONARD®
CORPORATION

7777 W. BLUEMOUND RD. P.O. BOX 13819 MILWAUKEE, WI 53213

Visit Hal Leonard Online at
www.halleonard.com

LEARN SOMETHING NEW EACH DAY

We know you're eager to play, but first we need to explain a few things. We'll make it brief...

Melody and Lyrics

You'll notice that the songs in this book look different from the "single line" music in *Harmonica 1*. That's because we've included the melody and lyrics to each song. That way, you can follow along more easily as you play your part—whether it's a blazing riff, a moving interlude, or the main melody. And if you happen to play with a singer, this new staff is their part.

New Rhythms

We're also going to lay some new rhythms on you this time around. Remember the quarter note? If you divide it into two, you get eighth notes. But what if you divide it into four? You get **sixteenth notes**, counted like this:

1 e & a   2 e & a   3 e & a   4 e & a

Now for a real puzzler: What if you divide a note into *three* equal parts? You get a **triplet**. Triplets are the basis of the lopsided "swing" or "shuffle" feel, which is very popular in blues and rock.

Sometimes, the shuffle feel is so strong, we change the time signature so that every beat is divisible by three. 12/8, for example, is a lot like 4/4, but each beat is felt as a dotted quarter note (♩.), which divides equally into three eighth notes. (No triplet necessary!)

As always, listen to the audio tracks to get a better idea of how these rhythms should sound!

4 beats per measure
dotted quarter (♩.) = one beat

Cool Tricks

You already know how to make your parts sound great with vibrato. Here's one more trick: the **shake**. A shake is a rapid alternation between two notes on adjacent holes of the harmonica. To play a shake, run the harmonica rapidly back-and-forth across your mouth, or shake your head back-and-forth (but please—not too hard!) while the harmonica stays put.

the shake

8vb and Loco

To make some of the harmonica parts easier to read, we've notated them up an octave (so you don't have to count so many ledger lines). These are marked with the indication **8vb**, which means, "play an octave lower than written." The **loco** indication tells you to resume playing normally (no, you're not crazy!).

If you're ever confused, just follow the blow and draw #'s. These never change!

Endings

Several of the songs have some interesting little symbols that represent different types of endings.

1st and 2nd Endings

These are indicated by brackets and numbers:

Simply play the song through to the first ending, then repeat back to the first repeat sign or the beginning of the song (whichever is the case). Play through the song again, but skip the first ending and play the second ending.

D.S., D.S.S., and D.S. al Coda

When you see the the initials "D.S.," go back and repeat from this symbol: 𝄋

When you see the the initials "D.S.S.," go back and repeat from this symbol: 𝄋𝄋

If either of these initials is followed by the phrase "al Coda," go back to the symbol (𝄋 or 𝄋𝄋) and play until you see the words "To Coda," then skip to the Coda (indicated by the symbol 𝄌) and finish the song.

Song Structure

Most songs have different sections, which may include any or all of the following:

 INTRODUCTION (or "intro"): This is a short section at the beginning that (you guessed it!) introduces the song to the listeners.

 VERSE: One of the main sections of the song is the **verse**. There will usually be several verses, all with the same music but each with different lyrics.

 CHORUS: Another main section of a song is the **chorus**. Again, there might be several choruses, but each chorus will usually have the same lyrics and music.

 BRIDGE: This section makes a transition from one part of a song to the next, or serves as a break between sections. For example, you may find a bridge between a chorus and a verse.

 SOLO (or INTERLUDE): This is your time to shine! Solos are often played over the verse or chorus structure, but in some songs the solo section has its own structure.

 OUTRO: Similar to the "intro," except that this section brings the song to an end.

That's about it! Enjoy the music...

Back at the Chicken Shack

By Jimmy Smith

Blowin' in the Wind

Words and Music by Bob Dylan

I'm Your Hoochie Coochie Man

Written by Willie Dixon

Love Me Do

Words and Music by John Lennon and Paul McCartney

love me do. _____

5↓   5↑   4↓ 3↑   3↑   3↑ 3↑ 3↑

G   1. C   2. G

5↓ 5↓ 5↓ 5↑   4↓ 3↑   3↑   3↑ 3↑   4↓ 3↑   3↑ 3↑ 3↑

Bridge

D   C   G

Some - one to love,   some - bo - dy new. _____

4↓   4↓   4↑   4↓
                             3↓

D   C   G   N.C.

Some - one to love,   some - one like you.

4↓   4↓   4↑   4↓
                             3↓

Verse

G   C   G   C

Love love me do. _____   You know I love you. _____   I'll

Miss You

Words and Music by Mick Jagger and Keith Richards

Piano Man

Words and Music by Billy Joel

There's an old   man_____   sit - tin'   next   to   me
And he's   talk - in' with   Da - vy who's   still in _____ the Na -

mak-in' love   to his   to - nic _____ and _____ gin.
vy   and pro - bab - ly   will   be   for   life.

Interlude

He says, _____
And   the wait -

Verse

"Son, can you_____   play me _____ a mem - o - ry? _____   I'm
- ress   is   prac - ti - cing _____ pol - i - tics_____   as   the bus

not real - ly_____   sure how   it   goes.   But it's
- iness - men   slow - ly get_____   stoned.   Yes,   they're

21

22

all in the mood____ for____ a mel-o-dy,_____ and

Interlude

you've got____ us feel-in' all____ right.

3rd Time to Coda ⊕   **Verse**

2. Now, John at the bar is a friend of mine.____
4. It's a pret-ty good _ crowd _ for a Sat-ur-day,____

He gets me my drinks for free.
and the man-a-ger ____ gives me a smile.   And he's
'Cause he

23

25

You Really Got Me

Words and Music by Ray Davies

Wonderful Tonight

Words and Music by Eric Clapton

29

*Fast*Track is the fastest way for beginners to learn to play the instrument they just bought. *Fast*Track is different from other method books: we've made our book/audio packs user-friendly with plenty of cool songs that make it easy and fun for players to teach themselves. Plus, the last section of the books have the same songs so that students can form a band and jam together. Songbooks for guitar, bass, keyboard and drums are all compatible, and feature eight songs. All packs include great play-along audio with a professional-sounding back-up band.

*Fast*Track Bass
by Blake Neely & Jeff Schroedl

Level 1
00264732	Method Book/Online Media	$14.99
00697284	Method Book/Online Audio	$7.99
00696404	Method Book/Online Audio + DVD	$14.99
00697289	Songbook 1/Online Audio	$12.99
00695368	Songbook 2/Online Audio	$12.99
00696440	Rock Songbook with CD	$12.99
00696058	DVD	$7.99

Level 2
00697294	Method Book/Online Audio	$9.99
00697298	Songbook 1/Online Audio	$12.99
00695369	Songbook 2/Online Audio	$12.99

*Fast*Track Drum
by Blake Neely & Rick Mattingly

Level 1
00264733	Method Book/Online Media	$14.99
00697285	Method Book/Online Audio	$7.99
00696405	Method Book/Online Audio + DVD	$14.99
00697290	Songbook 1/Online Audio	$12.99
00695367	Songbook 2/Online Audio	$12.99
00696441	Rock Songbook with CD	$12.99
00696059	DVD	$7.99

Level 2
00697295	Method Book/Online Audio	$9.99
00697299	Songbook 1/Online Audio	$12.99
00695371	Songbook 2/Online Audio	$12.99

*Fast*Track Guitar
For Electric or Acoustic Guitar, or Both
by Blake Neely & Jeff Schroedl

Level 1
00264731	Method Book/Online Media	$14.99
00697282	Method Book/Online Audio	$7.99
00696403	Method Book/Online Audio + DVD	$14.99
00697287	Songbook 1/Online Audio	$12.99
00695343	Songbook 2/Online Audio	$12.99
00696438	Rock Songbook with CD	$12.99
00696057	DVD	$7.99

Level 2
00697286	Method Book/Online Audio	$9.99
00697296	Songbook/Online Audio	$14.99

Chords & Scales
00697291	Book/Online Audio	$10.99

*Fast*Track Keyboard
For Electric Keyboard, Synthesizer or Piano
by Blake Neely & Gary Meisner

Level 1
00264734	Method Book/Online Media	$14.99
00697283	Method Book/Online Audio	$7.99
00696406	Method Book/Online Audio + DVD	$14.99
00697288	Songbook 1/Online Audio	$12.99
00696439	Rock Songbook with CD	$12.99
00696060	DVD	$7.99

Level 2
00697293	Method Book/Online Audio	$9.99

Chords & Scales
00697292	Book/Online Audio	$9.99

*Fast*Track Harmonica
by Blake Neely & Doug Downing

Level 1
00695407	Method Book/Online Audio	$7.99
00695958	Mini Method Book with CD	$7.95
00820016	Mini Method/CD + Harmonica	$12.99
00695574	Songbook/Online Audio	$12.99

Level 2
00695889	Method Book/Online Audio	$9.99
00695891	Songbook with CD	$12.99

*Fast*Track Lead Singer
by Blake Neely

Level 1
00695408	Method Book/Online Audio	$7.99
00695410	Songbook/Online Audio	$14.99

Level 2
00695890	Method Book/Online Audio	$9.95
00695892	Songbook with CD	$12.95

*Fast*Track Saxophone
by Blake Neely

Level 1
00695241	Method Book/Online Audio	$7.99
00695409	Songbook/Online Audio	$14.99

*Fast*Track Ukulele
by Chad Johnson

Level 1
00114417	Method Book/Online Audio	$7.99
00158671	Songbook/Online Audio	$12.99

Level 2
00275508	Method Book/Online Audio	$9.99

*Fast*Track Violin
by Patrick Clark

Level 1
00141262	Method Book/Online Audio	$7.99

HAL•LEONARD®

Visit Hal Leonard online at **www.halleonard.com**

0920
021

THE HAL LEONARD HARMONICA
METHOD AND SONGBOOKS

THE METHOD

THE HAL LEONARD COMPLETE HARMONICA METHOD — CHROMATIC HARMONICA

by Bobby Joe Holman

The only harmonica method to present the chromatic harmonica in 14 scales and modes in all 12 keys! This book will take beginners from the basics on through to the most advanced techniques available for the contemporary harmonica player. Each section contains appropriate songs and exercises that enable the player to quickly learn the various concepts presented. Every aspect of this versatile musical instrument is explored and explained in easy-to-understand detail with illustrations. The musical styles covered include traditional, blues, pop and rock.

00841286 Book/Online Audio............................. $12.99

THE HAL LEONARD COMPLETE HARMONICA METHOD — DIATONIC HARMONICA

by Bobby Joe Holman

The only harmonica method specific to the diatonic harmonica, covering all six positions. This book/audio pack contains over 20 songs and musical examples that take beginners from the basics on through to the most advanced techniques available for the contemporary harmonica player. Each section contains appropriate songs and exercises (which are demonstrated through the online video) that enable the player to quickly learn the various concepts presented. Every aspect of this versatile musical instrument is explored and explained in easy-to-understand detail with illustrations. The musical styles covered include traditional, blues, pop and rock.

00841285 Book/Online Audio............................. $12.99

THE SONGBOOKS

The Hal Leonard Harmonica Songbook series offers a wide variety of music especially tailored to the two-volume Hal Leonard Harmonica Method, but can be played by all harmonica players, diatonic and chromatic alike. All books include study and performance notes, and a guide to harmonica tablature. From classical themes to Christmas music, rock and roll to Broadway, there's something for everyone!

BROADWAY SONGS FOR HARMONICA   INCLUDES TAB
arranged by Bobby Joe Holman

19 show-stopping Broadway tunes for the harmonica. Songs include: Ain't Misbehavin' • Bali Ha'i • Camelot • Climb Ev'ry Mountain • Do-Re-Mi • Edelweiss • Give My Regards to Broadway • Hello, Dolly! • I've Grown Accustomed to Her Face • The Impossible Dream (The Quest) • Memory • Oklahoma • People • and more.

00820009 ....$9.95

CLASSICAL FAVORITES FOR HARMONICA   INCLUDES TAB
arranged by Bobby Joe Holman

18 famous classical melodies and themes, arranged for diatonic and chromatic players. Includes: By the Beautiful Blue Danube • Clair De Lune • The Flight of the Bumble Bee • Gypsy Rondo • Moonlight Sonata • Surprise Symphony • The Swan (Le Cygne) • Waltz of the Flowers • and more, plus a guide to harmonica tablature.

00820006..$10.99

MOVIE FAVORITES FOR HARMONICA   INCLUDES TAB
arranged by Bobby Joe Holman

19 songs from the silver screen, arranged for diatonic and chromatic harmonica. Includes: Alfie • Bless the Beasts and Children • Chim Chim Cher-ee • The Entertainer • Georgy Girl • Midnight Cowboy • Moon River • Picnic • Speak Softly, Love • Stormy Weather • Tenderly • Unchained Melody • What a Wonderful World • and more, plus a guide to harmonica tablature.

00820014 ....$9.95

HAL•LEONARD®

Visit Hal Leonard Online at
www.halleonard.com